X-TREME FACTS: SCIENCE

THE HUMAN BODY

by Catherine C. Finan

BEARPORT
PUBLISHING

Minneapolis, Minnesota

Credits:

Cover and title page, © SciePro/Shutterstock, © Alessandro De Maddalena/Shutterstock, © Pixel-Shot/Shutterstock, and © ixpert/Shutterstock; 4 top, zossia/Shutterstock; 4 top right, dragon_fang/Shutterstock; 4 bottom, 27 bottom middle, Syda Productions/Shutterstock; 5 top, Soru Epotok/Shutterstock; 5 top right, Happy Together/Shutterstock; 5 top left, Pommer Irina/Shutterstock; 5 bottom left, Anna Om/Shutterstock; 5 bottom center, Dragon Images/Shutterstock; 5 bottom right, Inside Creative House/Shutterstock; 6 top, sutadimages/Shutterstock; 6 middle, whitehoune/Shutterstock; 6 bottom, eurobanks/Shutterstock; 7 top, Breadmaker/Shutterstock; 7 top left, Khosro/Shutterstock; 7 top right, Nanette Dreyer/Shutterstock; 7 bottom, imtmphoto/Shutterstock; 7 bottom center, Asier Romero/Shutterstock; 8 top, Kichigin/Shutterstock; 8 bottom, Amelia Fox/Shutterstock; 9 top, Lapina/Shutterstock; 9 bottom left, Debbie Steinhausser/Shutterstock; 9 bottom right, Gelpi/Shutterstock; 10 top, santoelia/Shutterstock; 10 bottom, 11 bottom right, 12 bottom left, 14 left, 20 center, ViDI Studio/Shutterstock; 11 top left, ReaLiia/Shutterstock; 11 top right, pathdoc/Shutterstock; 11 bottom left, Hugo Felix/Shutterstock; 11 bottom center, adike/Shutterstock; 12 top, Romolo Tavani/Shutterstock;12 top left, Randall Reed/Shutterstock; 12 top right, Valentyna Chukhlyebova/Shutterstock; 12 bottom right, 21 bottom, Creativa Images/Shutterstock; 13 top, TonTectonix/Shutterstock; 13 top left, Jet Cat Studio/Shutterstock; 13 top right, ESB Professional/Shutterstock; 13 bottom, Martin Prochazkacz/Shutterstock; 13 bottom left, Vorawich/Shutterstock; 13 bottom left center, paffy/Shutterstock; 13 bottom right center, Dmitry Lobanov/Shutterstock;14 right, SciePro/Shutterstock; 15 top, LightField Studios/Shutterstock; 15 middle, hareluya/Shutterstock; 15 bottom left, Kamil Macniak/Shutterstock; 15 bottom right, fizkes/Shutterstock; 16 left, Kuznetsov Dmitriy/Shutterstock; 16 top, S K Chavan/Shutterstock; 17 top, wavebreakmedia/Shutterstock; 17 bottom, Bardocz Peter/Shutterstock; 17 bottom center, Donna Ellen Coleman/Shutterstock; 18 top, Nicolas Primola/Shutterstock; 18 bottom, DiversityStudio/Shutterstock; 19 top left, Michelle D. Milliman/Shutterstock; 19 top, Monkey Business Images/Shutterstock; 19 bottom left, Jeka/Shutterstock; 19 bottom center, Sergey85/Shutterstock; 19 bottom right, 23 top, New Africa/Shutterstock; 20 Tatjana Baibakova/Shutterstock; 20 bottom center, Liya Graphics/Shutterstock; 21 top, Breadmaker/Shutterstock; 21 top left, engagestock/Shutterstock; 21 top right, William Moss/Shutterstock; 22 top, SvetaZi/Shutterstock; 22 bottom left, Roman Samborskyi/Shutterstock; 22 bottom right pikselstock/Shutterstock; 23 top center, BlueRingMedia/Shutterstock; 23 bottom, msyaraafiq/Shutterstock.com; 24 bottom, Marko Poplasen/Shutterstock; 25 top, Odua Images/Shutterstock; 25 bottom, Everett Collection/Shutterstock; 25 bottom center, Oliver Denker/Shutterstock; 26 top, SAM PANTHAKY/AFP via Getty Images; 26 bottom, lunamarina/Shutterstock; 27 top, WENN Rights Ltd/Alamy Stock Photo; 27 bottom left, FGC/Shutterstock; 27 bottom right, Public Domain; 28 top, VectorMine/Shutterstock; 28 bottom left, Sergey Novikov/Shutterstock; 28 bottom right, Tropper2000/Shutterstock; 29 top left, Thongchai Pittayanon/Shutterstock; 29 bottom left, Zoart Studio/Shutterstock; 29 bottom left center, Nixx Photography/Shutterstock; 28-29, Austen Photography.

President: Jen Jenson
Director of Product Development: Spencer Brinker
Editor: Allison Juda

Produced for Bearport Publishing by BlueAppleWorks Inc.
Managing Editor for BlueAppleWorks: Melissa McClellan
Art Director: T.J. Choleva
Photo Research: Jane Reid

Library of Congress Cataloging-in-Publication Data

Names: Finan, Catherine C., 1972- author.
Title: The human body / Catherine C. Finan.
Description: Minneapolis, Minnesota : Bearport Publishing Company, [2021] |
   Series: X-treme facts: science | Includes bibliographical references and
   index.
Identifiers: LCCN 2020042976 (print) | LCCN 2020042977 (ebook) | ISBN
   9781647476748 (library binding) | ISBN 9781647476816 (paperback) | ISBN
   9781647476885 (ebook)
Subjects: LCSH: Human body—Juvenile literature.
Classification: LCC QP37 .F546 2021 (print) | LCC QP37 (ebook) | DDC
   612—dc23
LC record available at https://lccn.loc.gov/2020042976
LC ebook record available at https://lccn.loc.gov/2020042977

For more information, write to Bearport Publishing, 5357 Penn Avenue South, Minneapolis, MN 55419.
Printed in the United States of America.

Contents

Your Body Is Awesome

There's almost no end to the awesome things the human body can do. It can run, jump, sing, dance, juggle, and more. And every part of your body works together to make all of this activity happen. Your lungs are breathing. Your heart is sending blood and oxygen around your body. Your muscles are moving. And your brain is directing the whole show!

Your sneeze can be about 100 miles per hour (161 kph).

IT'S ALL THANKS TO YOU.

THAT'S SOME SPEEDY SNOT!

Allergies are nothing to sneeze at. They are your body's way of getting rid of stuff that doesn't belong!

CHECK OUT MY MIGHTY CHOMPERS!

The **enamel** on your teeth is the hardest part of your body. It's stronger than steel!

Your brain can be more active when you're asleep than when you're awake!

You're about 0.4 inches (1 cm) taller in the morning than you are at night. Blame it on **gravity!**

Your body makes more than a quart (1 L) of spit a day.

The Brain's the Boss

There's a gray lump of wrinkly **tissue** inside your skull. It may not look like much, but your brain is pretty powerful stuff! Your brain, spinal cord, and nerves make up the nervous system. The nervous system's job is to take in information from the outside world. Then, the brain decodes and reacts. It's the boss of you!

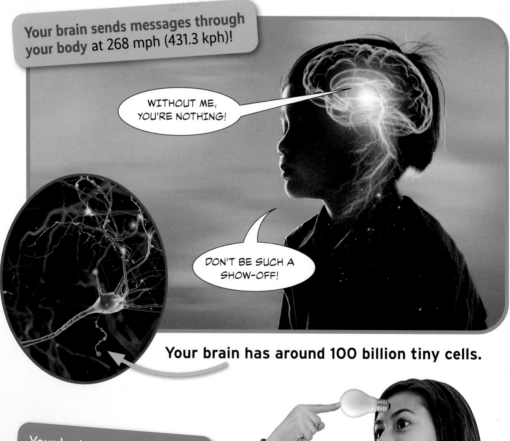

Your brain sends messages through your body at 268 mph (431.3 kph)!

WITHOUT ME, YOU'RE NOTHING!

DON'T BE SUCH A SHOW-OFF!

Your brain has around 100 billion tiny cells.

Your brain can make enough energy to power a light bulb!

LET'S SEE IF THIS WORKS.

Your brain isn't fully formed until you're about 25 years old.

Men's brains are about 10 percent bigger than women's. But brain size has nothing to do with intelligence!

A piece of brain tissue the size of a grain of sand has about 100,000 cells.

Super Senses

Your brain helps you take in the world through the five senses. Every time you see, smell, hear, taste, or touch something, your brain is sorting out messages and giving you sensory experiences. And it all happens almost instantaneously. Even though the brain's the boss, your super senses pack a pretty powerful punch.

All babies are color-blind at birth. They start seeing the colors red, orange, and green at about one week old.

Your taste buds die every few days, but new ones replace them almost as fast!

After eating a big meal, your hearing is worse for a short amount of time.

Your skin has four *million* sensory **receptors**!

About 80 percent of what we think is taste is actually smell!

Some people can't smell at all! They suffer from a condition called anosmia.

Marvelous Muscles

Your brain runs the show, and your senses help you experience the world. But without muscles, your body wouldn't get anything done! Your muscles are what make you move. Some muscles move because you tell them to, but others work without you having to think about them. These muscles keep your heart beating and food digesting . . . and even help control your poop! Let's see what makes muscles marvelous.

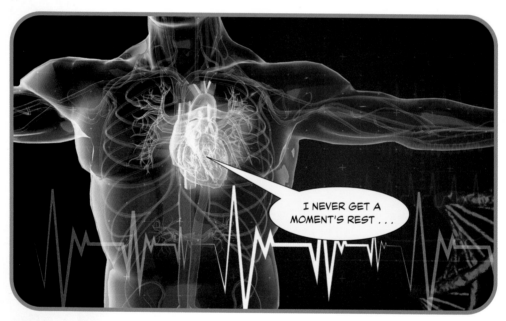

I NEVER GET A MOMENT'S REST . . .

Your body's hardest-working muscle is your heart. Every day, it beats about 100,000 times.

WHO SAID THAT?

BIGGER ISN'T ALWAYS BETTER, YOU KNOW.

Your two smallest muscles are inside your ear.

One of your body's strongest muscles is in your jaw. It lets you bite down with about 200 pounds (90.7 kg) of force!

11

Down to the Bones

Muscles get your body moving, but they can't do it alone. Skeletal muscles are attached to your bones, and they work together to put you in motion. Your skeleton is what gives your body form. Without these bones, you'd just be a big, fleshy pile of skin and muscle flopped out on the floor. Gross!

You're born with about 300 bones, but you have only 206 as an adult. Some of your bones join together as you grow.

WELL, I'VE GOT 206 BONES TO PICK WITH YOU!

I'VE GOT A BONE TO PICK WITH YOU.

I DARE YOU TO GRAB THE SKELETON'S FEMUR!

NO PROBLEM! IT'S NICE AND BIG!

The longest (and strongest) bone in your body is your femur, or thighbone.

Sit up straight—the 33 bones in your spine will thank you!

The stirrup bone in the ear is the body's smallest bone at 0.11 in (2.8 mm) long.

Babies have some bones that are made of **cartilage**— just like a shark's!

Hardworking Hearts

Bones help keep your **organs** safe inside your body. Your rib cage does this for your heart. And that's a good thing! Because your heart has enough to worry about. With each beat, it sends blood to every part of your body through blood vessels called arteries, veins, and capillaries. The process is repeated billions of times!

Your heart is in the middle of your chest just slightly to the left. It's about the size of your fist.

In an average lifetime, a person's heart will beat about 2.5 billion times!

NOTHING BEATS MY HEART'S BEAT!

Blood leaves the heart through arteries. One of those, the aorta, is as wide as a garden hose!

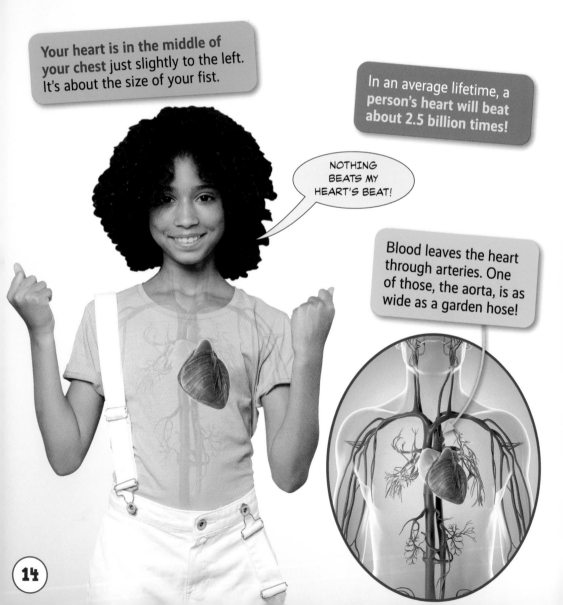

A human hair is 10 times thicker than some capillaries!

Capillaries are the smallest blood vessels in the body. They are just wide enough to let a single red blood cell fit through at a time.

No one knows for sure why **the heart is linked with the concept of love.**

Life-Giving Lungs

Breathing is the body's biggest team effort! When you breathe in, your lungs fill with air, and oxygen goes into your blood. Your heart then pumps the blood and the oxygen it carries around your body. A gas called **carbon dioxide** is drawn out of your blood and **expelled** by your lungs when you breathe out. Without the oxygen that your lungs and heart provide, your body can't survive!

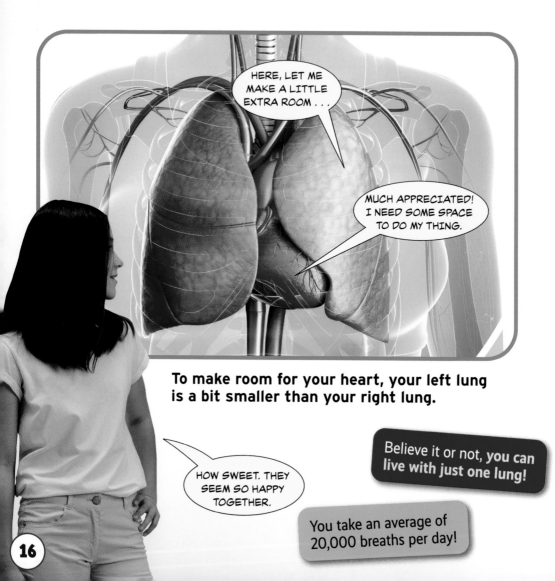

To make room for your heart, your left lung is a bit smaller than your right lung.

Believe it or not, **you can live with just one lung!**

You take an average of 20,000 breaths per day!

Each day, you breathe in more than 2,000 gallons (7,570 L) of air. That could fill up a swimming pool!

I'M OUT OF BREATH. IT'S TIME TO GET AN OXYGEN REFILL!

Most people can't hold their breath for longer than two minutes.

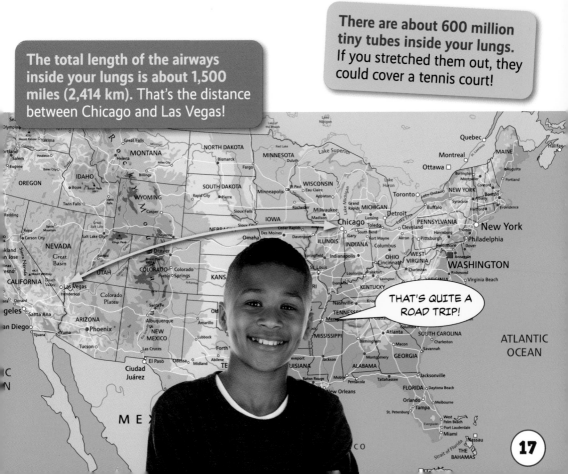

There are about 600 million tiny tubes inside your lungs. If you stretched them out, they could cover a tennis court!

The total length of the airways inside your lungs is about 1,500 miles (2,414 km). That's the distance between Chicago and Las Vegas!

THAT'S QUITE A ROAD TRIP!

Chew on This

Your body doesn't just need blood and oxygen. It also needs **nutrients**. Your teeth and stomach help break down food to get these nutrients. When you eat pizza, your teeth chew it into smaller bits, which mix with **saliva** to make swallowing easier. From there, muscles push the chewed pizza down your throat and into your stomach. **Gastric acid** in your stomach breaks it down even more. And that's just the beginning. . . .

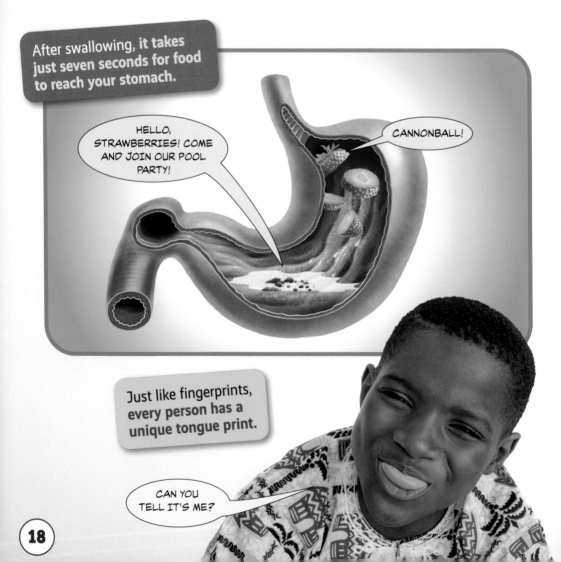

After swallowing, it takes just seven seconds for food to reach your stomach.

Just like fingerprints, every person has a unique tongue print.

You don't need gravity to move food to your stomach. You can eat upside down (but it's not recommended!).

The gastric acid in your stomach is the same kind of acid found in some toilet cleaners!

Your stomach makes about a half gallon (1.9 L) of gastric acid each day. Just one drop could eat through wood!

Out with It

The pizza in your stomach is ready for the next part of the trip—a slide through the long, twisted tunnel of your small intestine. This is where most of **digestion** takes place and where nutrients are **absorbed** into the blood. Any part of the food your body can't use goes to your large intestine. There, extra water is absorbed. What's left is . . . poop! And your body wants to get rid of it!

It takes about four hours for food to move through your small intestine.

MY LUNCH IS TAKING QUITE THE JOURNEY.

An adult's small intestine isn't small at all! It's about 22 feet (6.7 m) long.

You can live without your large intestine!

As they break down food, **bacteria** in your large intestine make gas. So, the next time you fart, blame your gut bacteria!

In total, we spend about a year of our lives sitting on the toilet!

Your poop is waste from food eaten yesterday—or even the day before that!

Keep It Clean

Your intestines absorb nutrients and get rid of poop, but you have other organs that also work hard to get rid of what your body doesn't need. Your liver is your largest **internal** organ. It filters blood from your digestive system, including any harmful chemicals. Your kidneys also filter blood, removing something called **urea**. This is one part of the pee that is stored in your bladder!

When it's full, your liver holds about 10 percent of all the blood in your body!

REGENERATION IS ONE OF MY MANY SUPERPOWERS!

Your liver is your only organ that can completely regenerate itself!

Your brain can't function without your liver.

WHAT'S WRONG WITH YOUR DAD?

OH, IT'S NOTHING. HIS LIVER IS ACTING UP AGAIN.

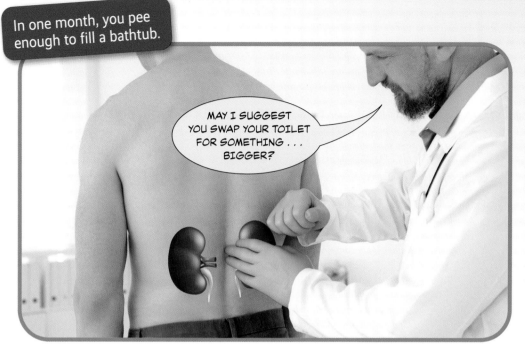

Your kidneys are responsible for producing urine.

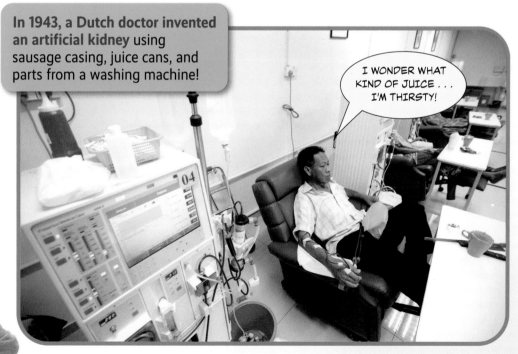

An artificial kidney takes the blood out of your body and filters it before returning it back to you.

More Than Skin Deep

The liver may be your biggest internal organ, but the largest organ of all covers your whole body. It's your skin! Your skin has the important job of protecting you and keeping everything where it needs to be. It keeps out germs and helps your body stay at the right temperature. It's also the reason you have a sense of touch. You could call it *sense*-ational!

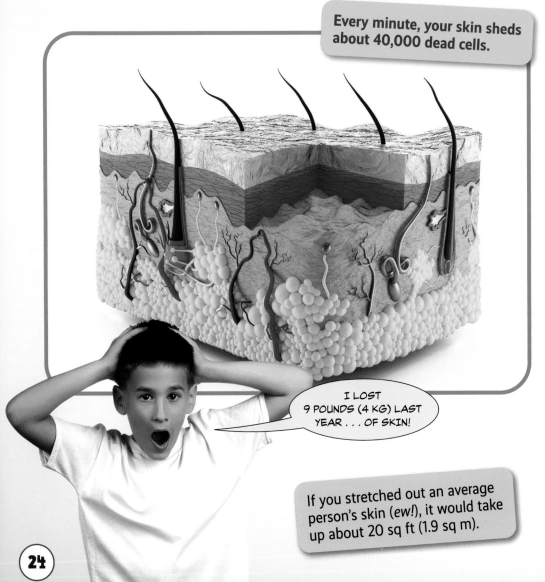

Every minute, your skin sheds about 40,000 dead cells.

I LOST 9 POUNDS (4 KG) LAST YEAR . . . OF SKIN!

If you stretched out an average person's skin (*ew!*), it would take up about 20 sq ft (1.9 sq m).

There are billions of bacteria, germs, and viruses living on your skin right this minute.

TAKE THAT, GERMS. I'LL SHOW YOU WHO'S THE BOSS HERE.

Washing hands and using hand sanitizers can help your skin keep the bad stuff out.

The ancient Egyptians put salt, meat, onions, and even moldy bread under the skin to heal wounds. Delicious!

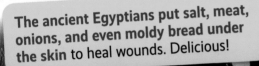

HOW IS MY FATHER?

HE'LL BE FINE. THE DOCTORS JUST GOT THE ONIONS READY.

Human Body Record Breakers

We've learned some pretty crazy facts about the human body. And if you think those were wild, there are some people whose bodies are even more extreme than the average person's. From the tallest people to the longest fingernails, the biggest mustache to the farthest eyeball pop, there are plenty of record-breaking stats that are truly impressive!

Francisco Domingo Joaquim is a bigmouth. Seriously! It stretches 6.7 in (17 cm) from end to end.

The longest mustache on record measured about 14 ft (4.3 m)!

BIG DEAL! HIS MUSTACHE IS LONG, BUT IT'S NOT AS COOL AS MINE!

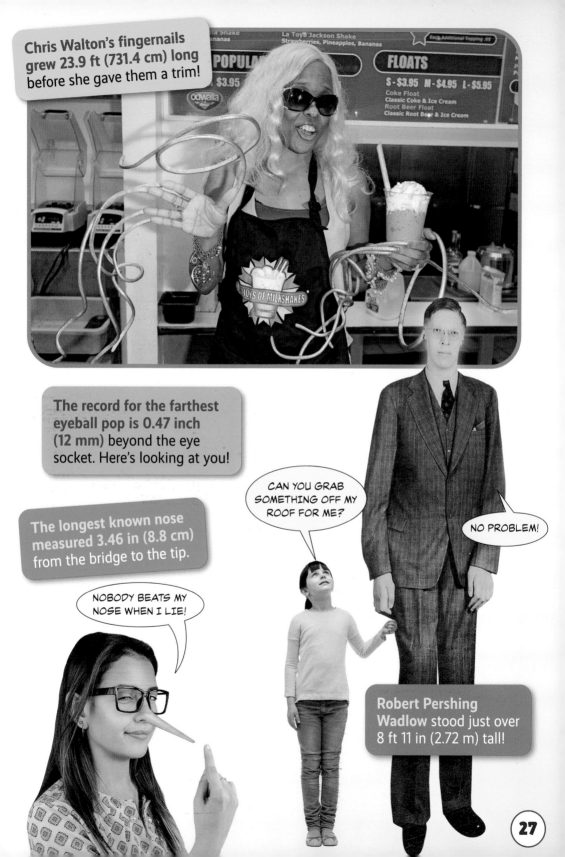

Chris Walton's fingernails grew 23.9 ft (731.4 cm) long before she gave them a trim!

The record for the farthest eyeball pop is 0.47 inch (12 mm) beyond the eye socket. Here's looking at you!

The longest known nose measured 3.46 in (8.8 cm) from the bridge to the tip.

NOBODY BEATS MY NOSE WHEN I LIE!

CAN YOU GRAB SOMETHING OFF MY ROOF FOR ME?

NO PROBLEM!

Robert Pershing Wadlow stood just over 8 ft 11 in (2.72 m) tall!

Model Brain
Activity

The brain is formed of two halves. Each half has four sections, called lobes, that control different things in your body. At the bottom of the brain are the cerebellum, which helps you move and balance, and the brain stem, which connects the brain to the spinal cord. Make a mushy model to learn more about the magnificent brain!

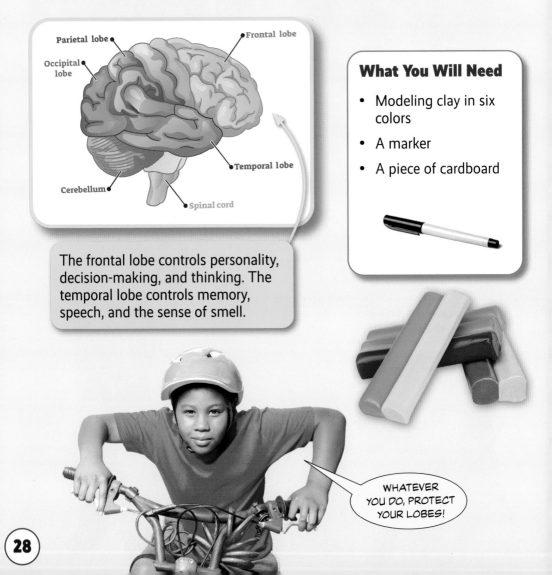

Parietal lobe

Occipital lobe

Frontal lobe

Temporal lobe

Cerebellum

Spinal cord

What You Will Need

- Modeling clay in six colors
- A marker
- A piece of cardboard

The frontal lobe controls personality, decision-making, and thinking. The temporal lobe controls memory, speech, and the sense of smell.

WHATEVER YOU DO, PROTECT YOUR LOBES!

Step One

Choose five colors of modeling clay to represent the different lobes and the cerebellum. Squish the clay in your hands to make it softer and then form it into small cylinder shapes.

Step Two

Roll each cylinder of clay into a long snake shape.

Step Three

Use your last color of clay as the brain stem and spinal cord. Roll the clay into a ball. Flatten the ball into a pancake shape. Then, remove some clay to make a tube coming from the shape.

Step Four

Use the marker to draw an outline of a human head on the cardboard. Place the brain stem piece on the cardboard. Take a snake shape and fill in a lobe section by twisting and turning the clay. Repeat with each section of the brain.

Glossary

absorbed taken in or soaked up

bacteria tiny, one-celled organisms

carbon dioxide a colorless, odorless gas made up of carbon and oxygen; we breathe out carbon dioxide

cartilage a strong white tissue that forms part of the skeleton of humans

digestion the process by which food is broken down into a simpler form after being eaten

enamel the hard, shiny covering of a tooth

expelled pushed or forced out

gastric acid a chemical in the stomach

gravity the force that draws all objects on Earth toward the ground

internal inside your body

nutrients things in food that help people live and grow

organs parts of the body that have certain jobs to do

receptors structures in the body, such as nerve endings, that pick up sensory information

regenerate to grow new tissue or parts to replace lost or injured tissue or parts

saliva spit

tissue a group of cells in the body that are like one another and do similar things

urea a substance that makes up part of urine

Read More

Braun, Eric. *Awesome, Disgusting, Unusual Facts about the Human Body (Hi Jink. Our Gross, Awesome World).* Mankato, MN: Black Rabbit Books, 2018.

Leed, Percy. *Guts: A Stomach-Turning Augmented Reality Experience (The Gross Human Body in Action).* Minneapolis: Lerner Publications, 2020.

Weird but True: Human Body: 300 Outrageous Facts About Your Awesome Anatomy (National Geographic Kids). Washington, D.C.: National Geographic, 2017.

Learn More Online

1. Go to **www.factsurfer.com**

2. Enter "**X-treme Human Body**" into the search box.

3. Click on the cover of this book to see a list of websites.

Index

About the Author

Catherine C. Finan is a writer living in northeastern Pennsylvania. She enjoys writing about a wide range of subjects—including the human body—but she can't stand the sight of blood!